THE
MEANING
OF
LIFE

it all hangs on ONE decision

R.J. Albanese

with E.T. Sherman

The Meaning of Life
it all hangs on ONE decision

ISBN 979-8-9867592-0-3
eBook ISBN 979-8-9867592-3-4
Copyright © 2014, 2024 R.J. Albanese and E.T Sherman
Second Edition
www.rjalbanese.com

contents

the point

I'm going to go straight to it. No trick
questions. No inspiring stories. I wrote this book
because I know the answer to the question, "What
is the meaning of life?" Although I studied many
disciplines like psychology, philosophy, and religion,
in the end it was a simple matter. To be up front,
everything I will write is based upon historical events
and truths found in the Bible.

Why did I choose the Bible? First, I studied the
religions of the world and realized the Bible was
entirely set apart from all other religious writings.
It was written in a miraculous way. It had to be
inspired by God because human beings just couldn't
have done it. The men who wrote the books in the
Bible were from different times and places, spanning

thousands of years, but the wording, the themes, and the imagery throughout the entire Bible are consistent.

That was not all. After doing the research I had to consider this: If you had in your hand a book that had been written centuries ago, a book about your life, and 90 percent of what had been predicted had happened exactly as this book had predicted, wouldn't you be just a little bit curious about everything else the book had to say about you? The Bible is such a book for all of us. More than 90 percent of the prophecies in the Bible concerning the history of mankind have been fulfilled *exactly* as written, and they were written thousands of years before most of them occurred.

When I say this book holds the key to the meaning of your life, I'm not being melodramatic. I'm serious. In fact, it is a matter of life and death — your eternal life or eternal death. It is also surprisingly simple. You will see for yourself. When all is said and done, the Bible presents a simple choice.

And you decide.

1
everything else

Consider what gives your life meaning in an "everyday" sense. Let's start with your appearance. Whether you are preparing for work or a social activity, no doubt you give a great deal of thought about how you look. If you place a high priority on looking good, you spend time, effort, and money to dress to impress. When you achieve that perfect look, it makes you feel good about yourself. Even if appearance is a lower priority, truly feeling good is important to everyone. Of course, there are exceptions.

There are a few uniquely disturbed souls who love darkness, depression, and continual anger or grief, but most of us want to feel good. Happiness and pleasure can be our greatest desires, becoming the most seductive drugs, and pursuing them can cause us to make some interesting decisions.

Your decisions determine the quality of your life. The sum total of the choices you make is what your life adds up to be. Each individual handles decision making differently, which leads us to how you think. What do you believe? In other words, what guides your decisions? Do you act impulsively, instinctively, or do you reason things out before you take a step forward?

Do you consult anyone or go it alone? Maybe it's important for you to be able to say, "I did it *my* way." Interestingly enough, how you think, believe, and decide has a lot to do with how you were taught by *others*, and most education does not teach you to think for yourself; it teaches you to believe what you are taught and make decisions to conform.

This leads us to go beyond your appearance, your feelings, and your thoughts, and place you in your culture. Your family, friends, religious affiliation (or not), educational institutions, profession, and any activities you pursue give you direct contact with your culture. Indirect contact comes through entertainment, books, magazines, television, the music you enjoy, and of course, the Internet. All of these things contribute significantly to who you are.

To elaborate further, you are raised in a societal structure where other humans tell you or model for you what is right or wrong, what is success or failure, and what is valuable or should be easily discarded. Culture is a powerful influence! It can determine what you believe gives meaning to your life.

Finally, there is your work and the things you do. These could be a profession and activities you get a great deal of satisfaction doing, or they could be drudgery. But is what you do who you are? Is your value as a person based on what you have achieved or the status you have obtained? Maybe for now. However, there will come a time when you won't do what you do anymore. What then? How will you value your life when things change?

And there it is. The problem with all of the above is *change!* Everyone and everything listed above is in a state of constant change.

- Your job may not exist in ten years.
- Your talents and abilities can lose their edge

and excitement.

- What is good or legal today can be evil and outlawed tomorrow.
- Your best friend or spouse can stand with you in one situation and betray you in another.
- The economy can make you a winner this year and a loser next year.
- You can get sick, have an accident — or grow old — and have less and less control about how you look, feel, and what you can do.
- And don't look to your feelings for any kind of validation! Your mood and attitude can change in a moment of time.

You know that none of the above has anything to do with the meaning of your life. To begin to unravel this all-important mystery, you need a deeper understanding of you.

Who are you, really?

2
YOU

The Bible says you are created in the image of God, who is a spirit. You probably sense you are a spirit, even if you have never thought about it. There is something inside your physical body that is YOU. Instinctively, you know YOU live in a physical body, like the air in a balloon. The balloon is dead and lifeless without the air in it; likewise, your body is dead without YOU in it. YOU are a spirit.

The Bible also says that YOU are eternal. YOU will live forever. There is life after the death of your physical body. YOU will leave your physical body when it dies and continue to live. The question is: Where will YOU go?

"Okay," you say, "I knew this was about religion."

Stay with me. That's not where we're going. All religions constitute a belief system of laws, traditions, and rituals. None of these will give you the meaning of life, especially when it comes to facing death of the body and the afterlife. Would you be interested to know that there is a way you can know for certain where you will spend eternity? Sounds impossible, but the Bible says you can absolutely know for sure.

Eternal truth about your eternal spirit will give YOU eternal security — and the meaning of life now and forever.

Since the Bible is all about eternal truth, let's go get some more.

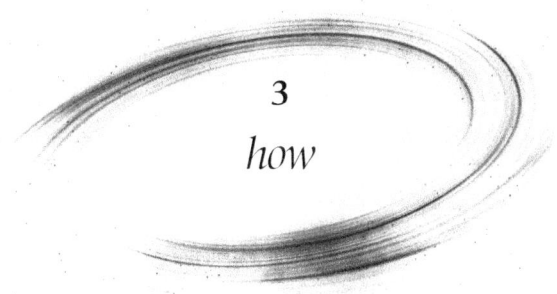

3

how

The Bible starts at the beginning of human history for a reason. God wanted us to know who we are. Knowing "how" we began gives us understanding about the meaning of our lives. Moreover, today scientists are seriously exploring the chromosomal evidence that all human beings are descended from one man and one woman, which is what the Bible tells us about our beginnings. You may have heard the story of Adam and Eve.

The Bible says God made Adam and Eve from the dust of the Earth and breathed His life or Spirit into them. So basically, human beings are spirits in dust! In the beginning, the "air" in our "balloon" was the very life of God, who never dies. That's why we are *eternal* spirits. His eternal Spirit made our spirits. In the beginning His Spirit also lived in our spirits, which means we were in continuous communication with the God of the universe — WOW!

I realize you may believe in the evolutionary theory (and, where the creation of humans is concerned, it is still a theory), that we began as a self-multiplying cell that grew in primordial ooze and eventually crawled onto dry land, adapting and mutating until we became like apes and then humanoids. There's one big problem with that theory: It doesn't give much meaning to your life.

If you get in touch with your eternal spirit, YOU will sense YOU can't be an accident of nature. YOU are created by design, and the Bible says that God designed YOU in His image and likeness. Since He is the essence of love and truth in the highest sense, YOU desire to embody love and truth in the highest sense. YOU can relate to Him! YOU can talk with Him and do things with Him. YOU can even get mad at Him when YOU don't understand what He's doing.

God created YOU to be a significant, unique, eternal spirit who communes with Him, the Creator of the Universe, spirit to Spirit. That gives YOU a lot of meaning!

And there's more.

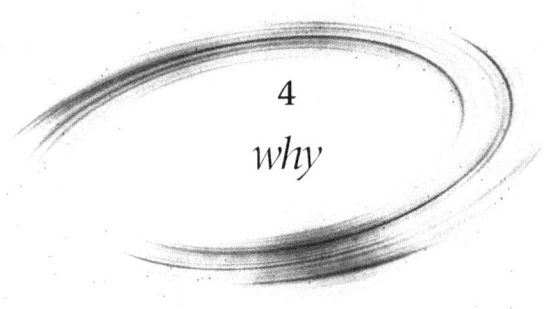

4
why

According to the Bible, "how" we were created gives us *eternal value*. "Why" we were created gives us *eternal purpose*. Our primary purpose is to fulfill God's deep desire to love and bless. Before He created Adam and Eve, He took six days to create the perfect environment, the beautiful and abundant Garden of Eden, which would be their home. Then, right after He breathed eternal life into them, He gave them a job. He knew, because He made them like Himself, they would want to express their love, creativity, and energy in significant ways. So He commanded them to be fruitful, to multiply, to subdue the Earth, and to have dominion over all the creatures of the Earth.

Understand: A command from God is not what

you might think. His commands are never cold and controlling. They always reflect His love and wisdom. His commands either give you the freedom to run with a task or warn you of something that will harm or destroy you. In the beginning, with Adam and Eve (i.e., the human race), He was doing both.

God commanded us to be fruitful, to bring His creative life and goodness into everything we do. Multiplying means God loves more of everything, especially children. Just think about it: He calls himself "Father." And subduing the Earth means bringing it under subjection. We are to rule it. This includes the creatures in the air, on the Earth, and in the water.

Now if the Earth needed to be ruled and subdued, there had to be someone or something Adam and Eve had to guard against. This was the warning part. We had an adversary on the Earth, and the Bible doesn't leave us hanging. It identifies our enemy as Satan, whose name means "the opposer of good." He's God's enemy and our enemy. This is important for you to know, because Satan hates all humans and is the most evil being in the universe. He's in the business of inspiring people to do terrible things to themselves and each other.

You may wonder, since the Bible says God created everything and everything He created was good, how did this evil being come to exist? The Bible answers this question. Before God created human beings, He created angels. Among them were three leaders, or archangels: Gabriel, Michael, and Lucifer. Gabriel is the messenger angel. Whenever God needs to send a message to someone, He sends Gabriel. Michael is His warrior angel. When He needs to do battle, Michael gets the call. Then there was Lucifer.

Lucifer was the angel of worship. His name means "light bearer," because worship to God produces light, both spiritual and physical. Worshipping God illuminates your soul, brings His heavenly presence on the scene, and actually changes the atmosphere in you and around you. You can relate to this when you think about the different kinds of music and how they affect you. You are going to have a totally different vibe in a rock concert than you have listening to a classical symphony.

With all his musical ability and talent, Lucifer was an amazing creature. We can only imagine what it was like when he conducted praise and worship to God.

Unfortunately, he began to see his beauty and talents as his own instead of gifts from his Creator. He chose to have pride in himself alone and rebelled against God, making the move to kick God off His throne and take His place! How crazy is that?

The chief worshipper of God became His chief enemy. Lucifer, the light bearer, became Satan, the prince of darkness. Therefore, Satan's self-appointed mission is to take everything God created and pervert it, twist it, and turn it to evil — including human beings. He watched God create Adam and Eve and give them dominion over the Earth, and it didn't take him long to launch his attack. He took the form of a serpent and invaded the Garden of Eden, the place God had charged Adam and Eve to guard and protect.

Adam and Eve always had drawn the meaning of their lives from their relationship with their Father God. He loved them, told them the truth, and entrusted them with the future of the Earth. Talk about meaning! Then an extremely intelligent and cunning creature entered their Garden and offered them an alternative lifestyle.

One decision changed everything.

5
fallen

When Lucifer rebelled and was literally thrown out of Heaven, the Bible says he fell like lightning from Heaven to Earth. He was the first to fall. Then came Adam. God had issued another command: They could eat the fruit of any tree in the Garden except one, the Tree of the Knowledge of Good and Evil. If they ate the fruit of that tree, they would die two deaths. First, they would die spiritually. Their spirit would be eternally separated from God. As a result of their spiritual death, their physical bodies would begin to die as well. That's why we call this the Tree of Death.

God also placed the Tree of Life in the Garden. If Adam and Eve had eaten the fruit of that tree and avoided the Tree of Death, mankind would have never known spiritual or physical death. We would have enjoyed the blessings of eternal life forever.

Two trees. Life and Death. An eternal choice.

That's extreme!

Why did God set this up? He created us like Him. He respects our right to choose. And He is good and just. He has a responsibility to keep any form of evil out of His kingdom, so He tests the hearts of each human being. Are we with Him or not? Do we want eternal life or eternal death?

As Adam and Eve looked from the Tree of Life to the Tree of Death, Satan came into the Garden of Eden in the body of a snake and did what he always does. He twisted God's words. He made God's command sound like He was denying them pleasure instead of warning them about the Tree of Death. Satan convinced them they would be missing something great if they obeyed God. This is how the devil gets people to sin, which is willfully and knowingly disobeying God.

Satan first deceived Eve into eating the fruit of the Tree of Death, so some men try to blame mankind's fall on women, but the Bible indicates Adam was somewhere nearby. The Bible also says that Eve was deceived, but Adam sinned with full knowledge of what he was doing. That's why God held the man responsible for the Fall of mankind.

Why didn't God stop them from sinning? Again, God couldn't interfere because He gave humans the right to choose. This is something the Bible makes abundantly clear: God respects your right to choose, even if you choose to be eternally separated from Him.

When Adam and Eve fell, God's warning came to pass: They died twice, first spiritually (immediately separated from God) and then physically (over a long period of time). How does it feel to die spiritually? We can only imagine the horror of it, but the Bible gives us some idea.

Before the Fall in the Garden, the Spirit of God was living in Adam and Eve. The power of God surrounded them. His glory was their clothing. They didn't even care that they were naked! They literally walked in perfection, only conscious of the love of God. In other words, they lacked all *self-consciousness* because they were 100 percent *God-conscious*.

After they sinned and died spiritually, the Spirit of God left them. They were separated from God and His power and glory — naked in this world — and became totally *self-conscious*. They were terrified, even of God, and ashamed. Adam and Eve immediately tried to cover their "nakedness" and hide from God.

Have you ever noticed how doing evil and sinning is always selfish and self-centered? You did wrong because you wanted to please yourself. And when you sin, you feel guilty, vulnerable, and afraid. You are sure everyone is looking at you and thinking badly of you, even if you know they have no idea what you thought, said, or did. That's because God knows and you know.

No matter how hard you struggle to live right, or how much success you achieve, you still manage to make mistakes and do the wrong thing from time to time. Maybe you finally gave up trying to be "good" and became a champion sinner. I personally know how that feels!

Sometimes hearing the truth is hard, but you are fallen. You didn't ask to be. But thanks to Adam and Eve...

You were born that way.

6
illegal

Born fallen? This can't be good! Did God make a mistake?

Let me tell you about the God of the Bible. He plainly states who He is and what is His endgame. He loves you unconditionally, which means no matter what you do, He still loves you. Even if you curse Him, reject Him, and vow to go to Hell to be away from Him forever, He still loves you. And He doesn't want to watch you from afar. He wants to be your closest friend and partner in life, to bless you beyond your wildest dreams.

Another thing about God — He's wise! The Bible says His thoughts and ways are higher than yours, but He wants you to know what is good and what is not; therefore, when He created the universe,

He established laws by which it would operate. These laws are good and just, because He is good and just. He wired the universe so that when you make a decision, you will experience the consequences of your decision. In this way, you discover what is right and what is wrong by *experience*.

Along with establishing laws, in His wisdom God created you with a conscience, so you can *instinctively* know what is right and wrong. The first time you lie, steal, or use the Lord's name in vain, something inside you reacts. Your action "pulls" against you. That is your conscience letting you know that you have violated a law of God — that you are illegal.

I said you *are* illegal because the Bible says you were born *wanting* to sin and rebel against God's law. This desire is called the sin nature. Every human being is born in this condition. If you don't believe it, just tell a toddler not to do something. You will see the sin nature come alive right before your eyes! Tell an adult, "This is illegal," and they will want to do it all the more. They have to fight themselves to keep from doing it.

There are a myriad of laws in the Bible, but the most famous ones are called the Ten Commandments. They give you the basics. Just these ten let you know a lot about what God says is illegal.

1. Don't have any other gods but Me.
2. Don't make a carved image of anything in the air, on the Earth, or in the water. Don't bow to them, serve them, or worship them.
3. Don't take the name of the Lord your God in vain: frivolously, or as a curse word.
4. Remember the Sabbath day, to keep it holy. You have six days to work, then the seventh you are to rest in Me. This will be a blessing to you and your household.
5. Honor your father and your mother. If you do this, you will live a long life in the land I give you.
6. Don't murder.
7. Don't commit adultery.
8. Don't steal.
9. Don't lie about anybody.
10. Don't crave or "lust after" anyone else's house, spouse, servants, or property.

How many of these have you broken? Did you feel good? How about the consequences of your actions — were they fun?

The Bible says that if you break any one law, you are guilty of breaking *all* of them. Remember, God is totally good. Absolutely no evil (and therefore no sinning) is allowed in His presence. Since you were born with a nature to sin, even if you try to keep every one of these laws, you will fail and stay separated from Him. There is something inside you that *wants* to break them — and your mind will go to great lengths to justify it. So God's laws reveal that you are totally in the illegal zone, and there is no way you can save yourself from you. You have a problem!

God also has a problem: According to His own laws, He cannot be close to you because you are a sinner. You are illegal. This grieves Him because He loves you and wants a close relationship with you. This is also a big problem for you if you want to hang out with God, really get to know Him, discover the eternal YOU, and go to Heaven.

Being wise and loving, God has an answer to your problem — and His!

7
the promise

Did you know God shed the first innocent blood on Earth? It was truly an act of love. He killed animals and used their skins to cover Adam and Eve's physical nakedness. Even after they disobeyed Him and sinned, He still loved them and wanted to protect them!

When God slaughtered these animals, He revealed more than the terrible price to cover their *physical* nakedness. He also showed them that only the shedding of innocent blood would restore them *spiritually*. It had to be a man's blood, because Adam was the one who sinned with his eyes wide open. Eve was deceived, but Adam knew he was sinning against God. The only thing that would pay for Adam's sin (and ours), make our spirits alive again, and restore us to the Father, was the blood of an innocent man.

Immediately after the Fall, God promised to send the Innocent One. He told Satan a man was coming, who would be born of the "seed of a *woman.*" This wording pops out at us because the Bible usually refers to "seed" as the seed of the *man.* God was hinting that this Innocent One would not have a human father. God would be the Father, and the mother would be a virgin.

God also declared that Satan's spiritual followers would wound the Innocent One (speaking of the crucifixion), but the Innocent One would crush Satan's head (speaking of the resurrection). Satan didn't understand the full meaning of God's words, but he was freaked out. He knew someone was coming to get him because God said it! Even Satan acknowledges the fact that God never lies and always keeps His word. As a result, the devil began to try to murder anyone he thought might be that Innocent One.

Satan's first target was Abel, Adam and Eve's firstborn, who was a really good son. Satan incited his brother Cain to get jealous and kill him. And he didn't stop there. Through the centuries he inspired fear, jealousy, and hatred in kings and leaders whenever there was the slightest chance the time was right for the Innocent One to be born. At these times, male babies were slaughtered. In ancient Egypt, he influenced Pharaoh to murder all male Jewish babies when Moses was born. By this time, Satan had figured out God had chosen the Jews to bring forth the Innocent One, the Messiah.

Finally, Satan prodded King Herod (the figurehead king of the Jews during the occupation of Israel by the Romans) to massacre all male Jewish babies under two years old in the region of Bethlehem, where Jesus of Nazareth was born. With the appearance of an unusually bright star, the witness of some shepherds, and the visit of some wise men from the East, Satan had finally located the Promise of God. The Innocent One was on the Earth!

This newborn Promise was the way to the meaning of life.

8
the way

Jesus of Nazareth was the Innocent One, the Son of God, born of a virgin in Bethlehem, just as the prophets predicted centuries beforehand. You have probably heard the Christmas story: Jesus was born in a stable, laid in a manger, and visited by shepherds after the angels appeared to them. It's a wonderful story, but it was far more than that. As the angels declared to the shepherds, it announced peace on Earth and *goodwill* from God to us.

Jesus had a physical body just like us, but His Spirit was not like ours. He wasn't born with the sin nature because His father was God. He was an extraordinary child, but He did not begin His ministry until He was thirty years old. Then He declared His mission: "I am the way, the truth, and the life. No one comes to the Father except through Me."

Jesus' mission was to become our way back to the Father and eternal life. This is why the true Christian experience is not found in religious structure; Christianity is the eternal-life *relationship* with the Father God and His Holy Spirit through Jesus the Redeemer.

How and why is Jesus "the way "— and the only way?

1. Jesus lived a completely sinless life. As the Son of God, He did not inherit the sin nature we inherited from Adam. He was pure and innocent, like Adam before the Fall. Although Jesus was tempted in every way a person can be tempted by Satan, unlike Adam and Eve and the rest of us, He chose not to sin. He qualified to be the perfect sacrifice: a sinless man who could pay the debt for Adam's (and all mankind's) sin. No other human being could make that claim.

2. Jesus gave His life willingly as an act of love. He was hated by the religious, betrayed by one of His disciples, deserted by everyone but a few, denied by one of His closest friends, mocked, severely beaten, scourged (whipped), nailed to a cross, and left to die with criminals. Ironically, by God's standards Jesus was the *only* human being who was *not* a criminal! He shed His innocent blood and cried, "Father, forgive them! They don't know what they're doing." He expressed His love and the love of the Father who sent Him, while enduring the most horrific pain to obtain forgiveness for our sins.

3. Jesus paid the full price for sin. When He became our sin on the Cross, the Holy Spirit left Jesus. His human spirit died, separating Him from the Father. Being dead spiritually, He then could die physically and descend into Hell.

4. Jesus was the first "born" from the dead. Because Jesus *himself* had never sinned, Satan could not hold Him and God had the legal right to breathe the Holy Spirit into Jesus' human spirit. Thus, Jesus was the first to be "born again" spiritually.

5. Jesus defeated Satan and rose from the dead. Now alive to God again, Jesus stripped Satan of all authority over believers and was physically resurrected from the dead.

6. **Jesus' blood satisfied God's Law.** He walked into Heaven and sprinkled His innocent blood on the mercy seat of God, signifying that the debt for the sin of mankind was legally paid in full. The Bible says the Father was fully satisfied. Justice was served upon the Innocent so the guilty could go free. What an amazing concept!

7. **Jesus appeared to over 500 people on Earth for many days.** They hugged Him, talked with Him, walked with Him, and ate with Him. They also saw the scars of His sacrifice on the Cross in His hands, feet, and side. The eyewitness accounts of this time are recorded, historical fact. He is alive!

8. **Jesus ascended to Heaven to sit at His Father's right hand.** As foretold, He was crucified at the Jewish feast of Passover, resurrected the third day, and then ascended before the Jewish feast of Pentecost — the perfect sacrifice in God's perfect timing, prophesied thousands of years ago. No human being has fulfilled biblical prophecy of the Messiah except Jesus of Nazareth.

9. **Jesus sent the Holy Spirit on the Day of Pentecost to live in and come in power upon those**

who believed in Him. The Church was born — not a religious institution but a spiritual relationship with God and one another. The Holy Spirit made these people spiritually ALIVE to God! Their dead spirits burst into eternal life as God's Holy Spirit came to live inside them forever. Their sins were forgiven! They were eternal spirits again! They knew the way back to the Father...

So they ran out to tell everyone the Truth they knew.

9
the truth

Before Jesus ascended to Heaven, He issued several commands. He told His disciples to travel throughout the world and share the Good News: *Anyone* could be born again spiritually! All sins were forgiven through His innocent blood. Jesus was the Way to the Father and eternal life. Then came his final command: They could not be a witness to the Truth without the power of the Holy Spirit. He told the believers, "Wait together in prayer. Don't leave Jerusalem until you are baptized in the Holy Spirit."

True to His word, He sent the Holy Spirit on the Day of Pentecost, and those first believers ran into the streets of Jerusalem so full of joy that everyone accused them of being drunk! They were drunk all right, but not with alcohol or wine. They had been immersed in the Spirit of God, and their hearts were overflowing with the love and power of Jesus. Now, all they wanted to do was tell others the Truth.

These disciples had not only *learned about* Truth; they had *experienced* the Truth — Jesus. The Truth had made them spiritually alive to God! They wanted their families, friends, and everyone they came across to experience the Truth also. God's desire had become their desire. Their passion was to see every man, woman, and child reject Hell and embrace Heaven, to be free of the fear of death forever. This is the absolute Truth believers carry inside them.

Of course, Satan is also doing everything he can to keep you from the Truth. Governments, groups, and individuals under his influence suppress any knowledge of or belief in the Bible or the God of the Bible — but especially Jesus. Many people talk freely about God and will even quote Bible verses, but few speak of *Jesus* with biblical and historical accuracy. Why? Because anyone who hears the facts about Him instinctively knows: Jesus is the embodiment of absolute Truth.

Satan knows that if you embrace absolute Truth, you will not fall for his lies. He is the master of deception, but living with Jesus the Truth exposes every falsehood and smoking mirror. I'd like to say that once you embrace the Truth, Satan leaves you alone, but he doesn't. The Good News is, when you live and walk in the Truth, the Holy Spirit inside you empowers and enlightens you. Through Him, you can defeat every evil attack and scheme the enemy throws at you!

Here's some more Good News: Jesus is the Living Word, so reading, studying, and meditating on the Bible is literally getting to know Him, the Truth. Frankly, this is something our natural minds can't fathom, but when you know Jesus through the Holy Spirit inside you, this experience of knowing the Truth is undeniable and life-changing.

Maybe you've heard people say that there is no such thing as absolute truth, because everything is relative and changing. This is one of Satan's best lies. After all, peace comes and goes. Hope is fleeting because of what might happen tomorrow. You are not absolutely certain about anything or anyone, so your life is built on shifting sand. Maybe that's why Jesus is called the *rock* of our salvation: He never changes, and we can count on Him, because He is *absolute* Truth.

Without real relationship with the Truth, Jesus, there are no certainties in life. The meaning of life will always be just beyond our grasp. If we reject the Truth, we will chase the value and purpose of our life elsewhere and never find it. We will be spiritually lost in a sea of vain thoughts, religious structures, or philosophical jargon. But the Truth — not just any truth spouted by us or someone else — can set us free. Only Jesus can unite us with the Father and reveal the meaning of our lives.

Embrace Jesus the Truth — and we embrace the Life.

10
the life

Jesus died a cruel death to give you a new life, but not life as you know it. He imparts eternal life, which is the greatest miracle you can experience. Some call it "getting religion," but that isn't even close to being true. When you receive eternal life, God infuses His very nature and power into your spirit. His eternal life makes you brand new. That's why Jesus called this experience being "born again."

One of the prophets of the Old Testament wrote about this experience as God showed it to him. He wrote that God would give people a new spirit and a new heart. The old spirit was dead to God, and the old heart was selfish and self-centered, wanting to sin and feeling condemned. The new spirit would be alive to God, doing life with Him. The new heart would desire to obey Him, not filled with terror and condemnation but overwhelmed with love and gratitude.

Jesus is the Life. The Life is a person just like you and me, except pure and holy. When we walk in the Life, the Holy Spirit inside our new, born-again spirit gives us supernatural ability to reject sin and to be pure and holy too. The Life that is Jesus changes everything! However, that doesn't mean the Life will be a bed of roses.

Christians may tell you that if you give your life to Jesus Christ, everything will be perfect. There is a real truth to that. Your dead spirit will be restored to eternal life as the Holy Spirit comes to live inside you. The Bible declares that your spirit is made absolutely perfect, which makes you righteous (right with God). And the best part is that the Holy Spirit is your constant companion. He teaches you, comforts you, guides you, corrects you, and empowers you through all of life's ups and downs. You will still experience difficulties in life, but *the Life* in you will get you through them.

When you are spiritually reborn, every area of your life is affected in awesome ways. God's love, power, and understanding will flow through your heart, your mind, your emotions, your will, your relationships, your profession, and how you conduct your life. You will really know without a doubt that you are going to Heaven! And the best part is *knowing* God, the Heavenly Father and Creator of the Universe. Just think about that for a while.

Life in Jesus is filled with unlimited possibilities when you know the Most High God has got your back! There are no words to describe the joy, fulfillment, and freedom you can experience simply by choosing the Way, embracing the Truth, and living the Life.

But you have to experience Him for yourself.

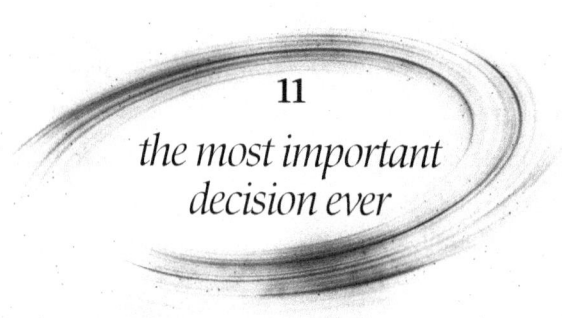

11

*the most important
decision ever*

The Way, the Truth, and the Life — as well as the history behind Him — is before you. The only thing standing between you and the eternal YOU, restored to God and walking in the full meaning of life, is a simple decision. It's so simple; many of our great minds have missed it. You simply...

> Believe in your heart that God raised Jesus from the dead, and confess with your mouth that Jesus is your Lord, and you will be saved.

Simple. But the ultimate in meaning!

God miraculously raised Jesus from the dead, and no other religious leader can claim that experience. The four Gospels of the Bible are historical, eyewitness accounts of the resurrection.

This is not hard to believe!

Jesus also did what the prophets of old said the Messiah would do. He shed His innocent blood in a cruel death to pay for your sins, purchase your forgiveness, and be the way back to the Father. He earned the right to be your Lord by giving His life for you. This is not rocket science!

Being filled with the love and life of God is simple yet profound. Simply believe Jesus was raised from the dead and confess to Him and to others that He is the Lord of your life. This decision is monumental because it will change your eternal destination! Instead of going to Hell under the condemnation of sin, you will live free forever in Heaven. You will enjoy the full meaning of life, eternal life — the God-kind of life!

What's more, Jesus stripped Satan of all authority over those who believe. If you have struggled with areas of sin or have been tormented in any way, as a child of God you can be free. Satan has no right to any aspect of your life unless you willingly give it to him. Through Jesus, you have complete authority over Satan and all demons. God threw them out of Heaven, and He wants to throw them out of your life too!

God has done His part by sacrificing His Son and raising Him from the dead. He has given you this book to point you to His Book, the Bible. You have all the necessary information to make a wise decision: Do you choose to continue eating the fruit of the Tree of Death, under Satan's influence, and destined for Hell — OR, will you partake of the Tree of Life, Jesus, and be spiritually born again, empowered by God's Spirit and destined to be with God for eternity?

Eternal death separated from God or eternal life with God?

It all hangs on one decision, so what do you want to do?

This is the most important decision you will ever make, but you might say, "Well, I don't have to make it *today*." No decision today means you are saying no to eternal life, and you have no guarantee you will see tomorrow. Remember, you can only make this decision while you are alive! Once you are dead, it's too late. That's why Jesus said again and again that *today* is the day of salvation.

If you are hesitating because you think, *I've gone too far and I've done things even God can't forgive,* be assured: Jesus paid for *every* sin and *all* sins — even yours — when He hung on the Cross. That's how much God wants you to receive forgiveness, to be free from any guilt about your past, and to experience the brand-new life He has for you.

Salvation in Jesus Christ is amazing! You can never be good enough to earn it or bad enough to be disqualified from it. He came for the sinner not the perfect, and we all qualify! All you have to do is say yes to the greatest gift you'll ever get from the Heavenly Father who loves you.

Now, if you are absolutely ready to receive God's free gift of salvation and declare Jesus is your Lord and Savior, but you don't know how to begin, it's as simple as praying what the Bible says:

God, I believe You sent Jesus to die for my sins and raised Him from the dead to give me a new spirit, a new heart, and a new life. *Today* and forever, I confess that Jesus is my Lord. Thank You for saving me! Amen.

This prayer is spiritual dynamite! If you meant it with all your heart, your prayer has blown up the kingdom of darkness in your life and flooded your whole being with the light and love of the Father. It is the greatest miracle a human being can experience.

If you are still undecided or skeptical about everything you have read, please do the research. Turn to "read it yourself" and allow God to speak to you. Again, don't take my word or anyone else's word. This is one decision that is solely between you and God. No one but you can decide your eternal destiny.

On the other hand, *if* you prayed the prayer, *then* I have more Good News for you.

12
if...then

If you have just believed in your heart that God raised Jesus from the dead and confessed to Him and to others that He is your Lord, the Bible says everyone in Heaven and all the angels are shouting for joy! You are a child of our Heavenly Father, a citizen of the kingdom of God, and a vital member of the Church, the body of Christ. You have a new family — all kinds of brothers, sisters, mothers, and fathers in the Lord — and they will be glad to meet you.

God wants you to have a pastor who will watch over you and see that you grow spiritually. The Bible says you need a pastor's care, which sometimes means correction and other times encouragement. You also need exposure to other leaders in the

Church. And you need to be around believers who will support you in friendship, in prayer, and in so many other ways. If you have ever felt alone and rejected, this new life may be a shock at first, but it will be a good shock! Being in a church is one of the ways you become more and more like Jesus.

How do you find the right church? Pray and ask God to show you where He wants you to be. He will lead you to a place where you feel at home, among those who will love you, teach you the Bible, and encourage you to obey the Holy Spirit. (He always knows what's best!) You will be free to grow in the gifts God has given you, while you are being challenged to mature in godly character.

Jesus also commanded believers to be baptized in water. Your pastor, representing God the Father, will lower you into the water, demonstrating that only God can save you. Symbolically, "going under" is dying to your old self with Jesus on the Cross, and "coming up" is being resurrected in Jesus. In water baptism, you show the world that you have a brand-new life in Him. This is an awesome experience!

You may have heard about an experience with

the Holy Spirit that includes speaking in tongues. Many believers around the world enjoy having a prayer language in which the Spirit prays through them in a powerful way, and they tell of being so much more effective in all God asks them to do. If you wish to have this experience, ask Jesus to baptize you in the Spirit as He did the disciples throughout the book of Acts, or talk to a pastor or another believer who has had this experience. The important thing is to receive all God wants to give you.

Your spiritual life will become fuller and richer if you set a time each day to pray (talk to God) and read the Bible, which is His Word *to you*. You stay strong physically because you exercise and eat healthy food, and you stay strong spiritually by spending time with God in prayer and studying His Word. And remember, you can commune with Him wherever you are and in whatever you are doing. He will bring meaning to every moment of your day!

You are going to find that Jesus will comfort you when you are struggling and correct you when you are wrong. He will love you when you are certain you are unlovable and give you wisdom for what

49

seems impossible. He will be everything you need! And He will see to it that you become the person you were created to be and do the things you were created to do.

The most important truth you should remember is, from this day through eternity, Jesus is your closest friend. He is your wisest counselor, smartest teacher, most discerning guide, abundant provider, highest line of defense — and greatest love. Moreover, His love and power have been deposited into your heart so you can be just like Him.

Now your mission is to share what you have received. Never allow this book to sit on a shelf! Keep giving it away! Jesus has commissioned you to pass on the Good News. Tell every man, woman, and child what you now know to be true: "It all hangs on one decision, and that decision will give you *The Meaning of Life!*"

read it yourself

Unless otherwise indicated, all scripture quotations are taken from the *New King James Version* of the Bible. Overall, I wanted to give you the most eloquent but still accurate verses, and sometimes that meant quoting other translations.

the point

Evidence That Demands a Verdict, by Josh McDowell, substantiates the uniqueness and historical authenticity of the Bible.

Amos 3:7 The Message
The fact is, God, the Master, does nothing without first telling his prophets the whole story.

2 • YOU

John 4:24
God *is* Spirit, and those who worship Him must worship in spirit and truth."

Hebrews 12:9 New International Version

Moreover, we have all had human fathers who disciplined us and we respected them for it. How much more should we submit to the Father of spirits and live!

Genesis 1:26-27

26 Then God said, "Let Us make man in Our image, according to Our likeness;...." 27 So God created man in His own image; in the image of God He created him; male and female He created them.

Ecclesiastes 12:5

For man goes to his eternal home,
And the mourners go about the streets.

3 • *how*

Genesis 2:7

7 And the Lord God formed man of the dust of the ground, and breathed into his nostrils the breath of life; and man became a living being.

Genesis 2:18, 21-23

18 And the Lord God said, "It is not good that man should be alone; I will make him a helper comparable to him."

21 And the Lord God caused a deep sleep to fall on Adam, and he slept; and He took one of his ribs, and closed up the flesh in its place. 22 Then the rib which the Lord God had taken from man He made into a woman, and He brought her to the man.

[23] And Adam said:
"This is now bone of my bones
And flesh of my flesh;
She shall be called Woman,
Because she was taken out of Man."

Genesis 3:20

And Adam called his wife's name Eve, because she was the mother of all living.

1 John 4:7-8

[7] Beloved, let us love one another, for love is of God; and everyone who loves is born of God and knows God. [8] He who does not love does not know God, for God is love.

Numbers 23:19 NEW LIVING TRANSLATION

God is not a man, so he does not lie.
He is not human, so he does not change his mind.
Has he ever spoken and failed to act?
Has he ever promised and not carried it through?

Psalm 119:160

The entirety of Your word *is* truth.

Ephesians 5:1 NEW LIVING TRANSLATION

Imitate God, therefore, in everything you do, because you are his dear children.

2 Corinthians 6:18

"I will be a Father to you,
And you shall be My sons and daughters,
Says the Lord Almighty."

4 • *why*

Genesis 1:26-31 NEW AMERICAN STANDARD BIBLE

²⁶ Then God said, "Let Us make man in Our image, according to Our likeness; and let them rule over the fish of the sea and over the birds of the sky and over the cattle and over all the earth, and over every creeping thing that creeps on the earth." ²⁷ God created man in His own image, in the image of God He created him; male and female He created them. ²⁸ God blessed them; and God said to them, "Be fruitful and multiply, and fill the earth, and subdue it; and rule over the fish of the sea and over the birds of the sky and over every living thing that moves on the earth." ²⁹ Then God said, "Behold, I have given you every plant yielding seed that is on the surface of all the earth, and every tree which has fruit yielding seed; it shall be food for you; ³⁰ and to every beast of the earth and to every bird of the sky and to every thing that moves on the earth which has life, *I have given* every green plant for food"; and it was so. ³¹ God saw all that He had made, and behold, it was very good. And there was evening and there was morning, the sixth day.

Genesis 2:8-9, 15-17

⁸ The Lord God planted a garden eastward in Eden, and there He put the man whom He had formed. ⁹ And out of the ground the Lord God made every tree grow that is pleasant to the sight and good for food. The tree of life was also in the midst of the garden, and the tree of the knowledge of good and evil.

¹⁵ Then the Lord God took the man and put him in the garden of Eden to tend and keep it. ¹⁶ And the Lord God commanded the man, saying, "Of every tree of the garden you may freely eat; ¹⁷ but of the tree of the knowledge of good and evil you shall not eat, for in the day that you eat of it you shall surely die."

Psalm 119:47

And I will delight myself in Your commandments, which I love.

Psalm 119:98

You, through Your commandments, make me wiser than my enemies; For they *are* ever with me.

Psalm 119:32

I will run the course of Your commandments, For You shall enlarge my heart.

Luke 1:19 NEW LIVING TRANSLATION

Then the angel said, "I am Gabriel! I stand in the very presence of God. It was he who sent me to bring you this good news!

Revelation 12:7-9 THE LIVING BIBLE

⁷ Then there was war in heaven; Michael and the angels under his command fought the Dragon and his hosts of fallen angels. ⁸ And the Dragon lost the battle and was forced from heaven. ⁹ This great Dragon—the ancient serpent called the devil, or Satan, the one deceiving the whole world—was thrown down onto the earth with all his army.

Isaiah 14:12-15

> [12] "How you are fallen from heaven,
> O Lucifer, son of the morning!
> *How* you are cut down to the ground,
> You who weakened the nations!
> [13] For you have said in your heart:
> 'I will ascend into heaven,
> I will exalt my throne above the stars of God;
> I will also sit on the mount of the congregation
> On the farthest sides of the north;
> [14] I will ascend above the heights of the clouds,
> I will be like the Most High.'
> [15] Yet you shall be brought down to Sheol,
> To the lowest depths of the Pit."

1 Peter 5:8

Be sober, be vigilant; because your adversary the devil walks about like a roaring lion, seeking whom he may devour.

5 • *fallen*

Genesis 2:8-9, 15-17

[8] The Lord God planted a garden eastward in Eden, and there He put the man whom He had formed. [9] And out of the ground the Lord God made every tree grow that is pleasant to the sight and good for food. The tree of life was also in the midst of the garden, and the tree of the knowledge of good and evil.

[15] Then the Lord God took the man and put him

in the garden of Eden to tend and keep it. [16] And the Lord God commanded the man, saying, "Of every tree of the garden you may freely eat; [17] but of the tree of the knowledge of good and evil you shall not eat, for in the day that you eat of it you shall surely die."

Deuteronomy 30:19

I call heaven and earth as witnesses today against you, *that* I have set before you life and death, blessing and cursing; therefore choose life, that both you and your descendants may live.

Genesis 3:1-13

[1] Now the serpent was more cunning than any beast of the field which the Lord God had made. And he said to the woman, "Has God indeed said, 'You shall not eat of every tree of the garden'?"

[2] And the woman said to the serpent, "We may eat the fruit of the trees of the garden; [3] but of the fruit of the tree which *is* in the midst of the garden, God has said, 'You shall not eat it, nor shall you touch it, lest you die.'"

[4] Then the serpent said to the woman, "You will not surely die. [5] For God knows that in the day you eat of it your eyes will be opened, and you will be like God, knowing good and evil."

[6] So when the woman saw that the tree *was* good for food, that it *was* pleasant to the eyes, and a tree desirable to make *one* wise, she took of its fruit and ate. She also gave to her husband with her, and he ate. [7] Then the eyes of both of them were opened, and they knew that they *were* naked; and they sewed

fig leaves together and made themselves coverings.

⁸ And they heard the sound of the Lord God walking in the garden in the cool of the day, and Adam and his wife hid themselves from the presence of the Lord God among the trees of the garden.

⁹ Then the Lord God called to Adam and said to him, "Where *are* you?"

¹⁰ So he said, "I heard Your voice in the garden, and I was afraid because I was naked; and I hid myself."

¹¹ And He said, "Who told you that you *were* naked? Have you eaten from the tree of which I commanded you that you should not eat?"

¹² Then the man said, "The woman whom You gave *to be* with me, she gave me of the tree, and I ate."

¹³ And the Lord God said to the woman, "What *is* this you have done?"

The woman said, "The serpent deceived me, and I ate."

Ephesians 2:2-3 New Living Translation

² You used to live in sin, just like the rest of the world, obeying the devil—the commander of the powers in the unseen world. He is the spirit at work in the hearts of those who refuse to obey God. ³ All of us used to live that way, following the passionate desires and inclinations of our sinful nature.

Psalm 51:5

Behold, I was brought forth in iniquity,
And in sin my mother conceived me.

6 • *illegal*

Jeremiah 31:3

> The Lord has appeared of old to me, *saying:*
> "Yes, I have loved you with an everlasting love;
> Therefore with lovingkindness I have drawn you.

1 John 4:16

> And we have known and believed the love that
> God has for us. God is love, and he who abides in
> love abides in God, and God in him.

Isaiah 55:8-9

> [8] "For My thoughts *are* not your thoughts,
> Nor *are* your ways My ways," says the Lord.
> [9] "For *as* the heavens are higher than the earth,
> So are My ways higher than your ways,
> And My thoughts than your thoughts."

Galatians 6:7-8

> [7] Do not be deceived, God is not mocked;
> for whatever a man sows, that he will also reap. [8]
> For he who sows to his flesh will of the flesh reap
> corruption, but he who sows to the Spirit will of the
> Spirit reap everlasting life.

Romans 2:14-15 New Living Translation

> [14] Even Gentiles, who do not have God's
> written law, show that they know his law when they
> instinctively obey it, even without having heard it. [15]
> They demonstrate that God's law is written in their
> hearts, for their own conscience and thoughts either
> accuse them or tell them they are doing right.

Exodus 20:3-17

³ "You shall have no other gods before Me.

⁴ "You shall not make for yourself a carved image—any likeness *of anything* that *is* in heaven above, or that *is* in the earth beneath, or that *is* in the water under the earth; ⁵ you shall not bow down to them nor serve them. For I, the Lord your God, *am* a jealous God, visiting the iniquity of the fathers upon the children to the third and fourth *generations* of those who hate Me, ⁶ but showing mercy to thousands, to those who love Me and keep My commandments.

⁷ "You shall not take the name of the Lord your God in vain, for the Lord will not hold *him* guiltless who takes His name in vain.

⁸ "Remember the Sabbath day, to keep it holy. ⁹ Six days you shall labor and do all your work, ¹⁰ but the seventh day *is* the Sabbath of the Lord your God. *In it* you shall do no work: you, nor your son, nor your daughter, nor your male servant, nor your female servant, nor your cattle, nor your stranger who *is* within your gates. ¹¹ For *in* six days the Lord made the heavens and the earth, the sea, and all that *is* in them, and rested the seventh day. Therefore the Lord blessed the Sabbath day and hallowed it.

¹² "Honor your father and your mother, that your days may be long upon the land which the Lord your God is giving you.

¹³ "You shall not murder.

¹⁴ "You shall not commit adultery.

¹⁵ "You shall not steal.

¹⁶ "You shall not bear false witness against your neighbor.

¹⁷ "You shall not covet your neighbor's house; you shall not covet your neighbor's wife, nor his male servant, nor his female servant, nor his ox, nor his donkey, nor anything that *is* your neighbor's."

James 2:10

For whoever shall keep the whole law, and yet stumble in one *point,* he is guilty of all.

Romans 7:15-24 New Living Translation

¹⁵ I don't really understand myself, for I want to do what is right, but I don't do it. Instead, I do what I hate. ¹⁶ But if I know that what I am doing is wrong, this shows that I agree that the law is good. ¹⁷ So I am not the one doing wrong; it is sin living in me that does it.

¹⁸ And I know that nothing good lives in me, that is, in my sinful nature. I want to do what is right, but I can't. ¹⁹ I want to do what is good, but I don't. I don't want to do what is wrong, but I do it anyway. ²⁰ But if I do what I don't want to do, I am not really the one doing wrong; it is sin living in me that does it.

²¹ I have discovered this principle of life—that when I want to do what is right, I inevitably do what is wrong. ²² I love God's law with all my heart. ²³ But there is another power within me that is at war with my mind. This power makes me a slave to the sin that is still within me. ²⁴ Oh, what a miserable person I am! Who will free me from this life that is dominated by sin and death?

7 • *the promise*

Genesis 3:7, 21 New Living Translation

⁷ At that moment their eyes were opened, and they suddenly felt shame at their nakedness. So they sewed fig leaves together to cover themselves.

²¹ And the Lord God made clothing from animal skins for Adam and his wife.

Hebrews 9:22 New Living Translation

For without the shedding of blood, there is no forgiveness.

1 John 1:7

The blood of Jesus Christ His Son cleanses us from all sin.

Genesis 3:14-15

¹⁴ So the Lord God said to the serpent:
"Because you have done this,
You *are* cursed more than all cattle,
And more than every beast of the field;
On your belly you shall go,
And you shall eat dust
All the days of your life.
¹⁵ And I will put enmity
Between you and the woman,
And between your seed and her Seed;
He shall bruise your head,
And you shall bruise His heel."

Isaiah 7:14 The Living Bible

A child shall be born to a virgin! And she shall call him Immanuel (meaning, "God is with us").

Luke 1:26-35

²⁶ Now in the sixth month the angel Gabriel was sent by God to a city of Galilee named Nazareth, ²⁷ to a virgin betrothed to a man whose name was Joseph, of the house of David. The virgin's name *was* Mary. ²⁸ And having come in, the angel said to her, "Rejoice, highly favored *one,* the Lord *is* with you; blessed *are* you among women!"

²⁹ But when she saw *him,* she was troubled at his saying, and considered what manner of greeting this was. ³⁰ Then the angel said to her, "Do not be afraid, Mary, for you have found favor with God. ³¹ And behold, you will conceive in your womb and bring forth a Son, and shall call His name Jesus. ³² He will be great, and will be called the Son of the Highest; and the Lord God will give Him the throne of His father David. ³³ And He will reign over the house of Jacob forever, and of His kingdom there will be no end."

³⁴ Then Mary said to the angel, "How can this be, since I do not know a man?"

³⁵ And the angel answered and said to her, "*The* Holy Spirit will come upon you, and the power of the Highest will overshadow you; therefore, also, that Holy One who is to be born will be called the Son of God.

Genesis 4:1-8

¹ Now Adam knew Eve his wife, and she conceived and bore Cain, and said, "I have acquired a man from the Lord." ² Then she bore again, this

time his brother Abel. Now Abel was a keeper of sheep, but Cain was a tiller of the ground. ³ And in the process of time it came to pass that Cain brought an offering of the fruit of the ground to the Lord. ⁴ Abel also brought of the firstborn of his flock and of their fat. And the Lord respected Abel and his offering,

⁵ but He did not respect Cain and his offering. And Cain was very angry, and his countenance fell.

⁶ So the Lord said to Cain, "Why are you angry? And why has your countenance fallen? ⁷ If you do well, will you not be accepted? And if you do not do well, sin lies at the door. And its desire *is* for you, but you should rule over it."

⁸ Now Cain talked with Abel his brother; and it came to pass, when they were in the field, that Cain rose up against Abel his brother and killed him.

Exodus 1:15-16

¹⁵ Then the king of Egypt spoke to the Hebrew midwives, of whom the name of one *was* Shiphrah and the name of the other Puah; ¹⁶ and he said, "When you do the duties of a midwife for the Hebrew women, and see *them* on the birthstools, if it *is* a son, then you shall kill him; but if it *is* a daughter, then she shall live."

Matthew 2

¹ Now after Jesus was born in Bethlehem of Judea in the days of Herod the king, behold, wise men from the East came to Jerusalem, ² saying, "Where is He who has been born King of the Jews? For we have seen His

star in the East and have come to worship Him."

³ When Herod the king heard *this*, he was troubled, and all Jerusalem with him. ⁴ And when he had gathered all the chief priests and scribes of the people together, he inquired of them where the Christ was to be born.

⁵ So they said to him, "In Bethlehem of Judea, for thus it is written by the prophet:

⁶ 'But you, Bethlehem, *in* the land of Judah,
Are not the least among the rulers of Judah;
For out of you shall come a Ruler
Who will shepherd My people Israel.'"

⁷ Then Herod, when he had secretly called the wise men, determined from them what time the star appeared. ⁸ And he sent them to Bethlehem and said, "Go and search carefully for the young Child, and when you have found *Him*, bring back word to me, that I may come and worship Him also."

⁹ When they heard the king, they departed; and behold, the star which they had seen in the East went before them, till it came and stood over where the young Child was. ¹⁰ When they saw the star, they rejoiced with exceedingly great joy. ¹¹ And when they had come into the house, they saw the young Child with Mary His mother, and fell down and worshiped Him. And when they had opened their treasures, they presented gifts to Him: gold, frankincense, and myrrh.

¹² Then, being divinely warned in a dream that they should not return to Herod, they departed for

their own country another way.

¹³ Now when they had departed, behold, an angel of the Lord appeared to Joseph in a dream, saying, "Arise, take the young Child and His mother, flee to Egypt, and stay there until I bring you word; for Herod will seek the young Child to destroy Him."

¹⁴ When he arose, he took the young Child and His mother by night and departed for Egypt, ¹⁵ and was there until the death of Herod, that it might be fulfilled which was spoken by the Lord through the prophet, saying, "Out of Egypt I called My Son."

¹⁶ Then Herod, when he saw that he was deceived by the wise men, was exceedingly angry; and he sent forth and put to death all the male children who were in Bethlehem and in all its districts, from two years old and under, according to the time which he had determined from the wise men.

¹⁷ Then was fulfilled what was spoken by Jeremiah the prophet, saying:

¹⁸ "A voice was heard in Ramah,
Lamentation, weeping, and great mourning,
Rachel weeping *for* her children,
Refusing to be comforted,
Because they are no more."

¹⁹ Now when Herod was dead, behold, an angel of the Lord appeared in a dream to Joseph in Egypt, ²⁰ saying, "Arise, take the young Child and His mother, and go to the land of Israel, for those who

sought the young Child's life are dead." [21] Then he arose, took the young Child and His mother, and came into the land of Israel.

[22] But when he heard that Archelaus was reigning over Judea instead of his father Herod, he was afraid to go there. And being warned by God in a dream, he turned aside into the region of Galilee. [23] And he came and dwelt in a city called Nazareth, that it might be fulfilled which was spoken by the prophets, "He shall be called a Nazarene."

8 • *the way*

Luke 2:1-20, 40-52

[1] And it came to pass in those days *that* a decree went out from Caesar Augustus that all the world should be registered. [2] This census first took place while Quirinius was governing Syria. [3] So all went to be registered, everyone to his own city.

[4] Joseph also went up from Galilee, out of the city of Nazareth, into Judea, to the city of David, which is called Bethlehem, because he was of the house and lineage of David, [5] to be registered with Mary, his betrothed wife, who was with child. [6] So it was, that while they were there, the days were completed for her to be delivered. [7] And she brought forth her firstborn Son, and wrapped Him in swaddling cloths, and laid Him in a manger, because there was no room for them in the inn.

[8] Now there were in the same country shepherds

living out in the fields, keeping watch over their flock by night. [9] And behold, an angel of the Lord stood before them, and the glory of the Lord shone around them, and they were greatly afraid. [10] Then the angel said to them, "Do not be afraid, for behold, I bring you good tidings of great joy which will be to all people. [11] For there is born to you this day in the city of David a Savior, who is Christ the Lord. [12] And this *will be* the sign to you: You will find a Babe wrapped in swaddling cloths, lying in a manger."

[13] And suddenly there was with the angel a multitude of the heavenly host praising God and saying:

[14] "Glory to God in the highest,

And on earth peace, goodwill toward men!"

[15] So it was, when the angels had gone away from them into heaven, that the shepherds said to one another, "Let us now go to Bethlehem and see this thing that has come to pass, which the Lord has made known to us." [16] And they came with haste and found Mary and Joseph, and the Babe lying in a manger. [17] Now when they had seen *Him*, they made widely known the saying which was told them concerning this Child. [18] And all those who heard *it* marveled at those things which were told them by the shepherds. [19] But Mary kept all these things and pondered *them* in her heart. [20] Then the shepherds returned, glorifying and praising God for all the things that they had heard and seen, as it was told them.

⁴⁰ And the Child grew and became strong in spirit, filled with wisdom; and the grace of God was upon Him.

⁴¹ His parents went to Jerusalem every year at the Feast of the Passover. ⁴² And when He was twelve years old, they went up to Jerusalem according to the custom of the feast. ⁴³ When they had finished the days, as they returned, the Boy Jesus lingered behind in Jerusalem. And Joseph and His mother did not know *it;* ⁴⁴ but supposing Him to have been in the company, they went a day's journey, and sought Him among *their* relatives and acquaintances. ⁴⁵ So when they did not find Him, they returned to Jerusalem, seeking Him. ⁴⁶ Now so it was *that* after three days they found Him in the temple, sitting in the midst of the teachers, both listening to them and asking them questions. ⁴⁷ And all who heard Him were astonished at His understanding and answers. ⁴⁸ So when they saw Him, they were amazed; and His mother said to Him, "Son, why have You done this to us? Look, Your father and I have sought You anxiously."

⁴⁹ And He said to them, "Why did you seek Me? Did you not know that I must be about My Father's business?" ⁵⁰ But they did not understand the statement which He spoke to them.

⁵¹ Then He went down with them and came to Nazareth, and was subject to them, but His mother kept all these things in her heart. ⁵² And Jesus increased in wisdom and stature, and in favor with God and men.

John 14:6

Jesus said to him, "I am the way, the truth, and the life. No one comes to the Father except through Me."

Hebrews 4:15

[Jesus] was in all *points* tempted as *we are, yet* without sin.

John 10:17-18

[17] "Therefore My Father loves Me, because I lay down My life that I may take it again. [18] No one takes it from Me, but I lay it down of Myself. I have power to lay it down, and I have power to take it again. This command I have received from My Father."

John 15:13

"Greater love has no one than this, than to lay down one's life for his friends."

Hebrews 2:14-15

[14] Inasmuch then as the children have partaken of flesh and blood, He Himself likewise shared in the same, that through death He might destroy him who had the power of death, that is, the devil, [15] and release those who through fear of death were all their lifetime subject to bondage.

Luke 16:19-23

[19] "There was a certain rich man who was clothed in purple and fine linen and fared sumptuously every day. [20] But there was a certain beggar named Lazarus, full of sores, who was laid at his gate, [21] desiring to be fed with the crumbs which

fell from the rich man's table. Moreover the dogs came and licked his sores. ²² So it was that the beggar died, and was carried by the angels to Abraham's bosom. The rich man also died and was buried. ²³ And being in torments in Hades, he lifted up his eyes and saw Abraham afar off, and Lazarus in his bosom."

Ephesians 4:8 New Living Translation

"When he ascended to the heights,
he led a crowd of captives
and gave gifts to his people."

Matthew 27:50-53 New Living Translation

⁵⁰ Then Jesus shouted out again, and he released his spirit. ⁵¹ At that moment the curtain in the sanctuary of the Temple was torn in two, from top to bottom. The earth shook, rocks split apart, ⁵² and tombs opened. The bodies of many godly men and women who had died were raised from the dead. ⁵³ They left the cemetery after Jesus' resurrection, went into the holy city of Jerusalem, and appeared to many people.

Colossians 1:18 New American Standard Bible

He is also the head of the body, the church; and He is the beginning, the firstborn from the dead, so that He Himself will come to have first place in everything.

Hebrews 9:11-12 New Living Translation

¹¹ So Christ has now become the High Priest over all the good things that have come. He has

entered that greater, more perfect Tabernacle in heaven, which was not made by human hands and is not part of this created world. [12] With his own blood—not the blood of goats and calves—he entered the Most Holy Place once for all time and secured our redemption forever.

1 Corinthians 15:3-6

[3] For I delivered to you first of all that which I also received: that Christ died for our sins according to the Scriptures, [4] and that He was buried, and that He rose again the third day according to the Scriptures, [5] and that He was seen by Cephas, then by the twelve. [6] After that He was seen by over five hundred brethren at once, of whom the greater part remain to the present, but some have fallen asleep.

Romans 8:34

It is Christ who died, and furthermore is also risen, who is even at the right hand of God, who also makes intercession for us.

You can read the other Gospel accounts of Jesus of Nazareth's trial, death, burial, and resurrection: Mark 14-16, Luke 22-24, and John 18-20. Here is the account in the Gospel of Matthew, chapters 26-28:

Matthew 26 New American Standard Bible

[1] When Jesus had finished all these words, He said to His disciples, [2] "You know that after two days the Passover is coming, and the Son of Man is *to be* handed over for crucifixion."

[3] Then the chief priests and the elders of the

people were gathered together in the court of the high priest, named Caiaphas; 4 and they plotted together to seize Jesus by stealth and kill Him. 5 But they were saying, "Not during the festival, otherwise a riot might occur among the people."

6 Now when Jesus was in Bethany, at the home of Simon the leper, 7 a woman came to Him with an alabaster vial of very costly perfume, and she poured it on His head as He reclined *at the table*. 8 But the disciples were indignant when they saw *this*, and said, "Why this waste? 9 For this *perfume* might have been sold for a high price and *the money* given to the poor." 10 But Jesus, aware of this, said to them, "Why do you bother the woman? For she has done a good deed to Me. 11 For you always have the poor with you; but you do not always have Me. 12 For when she poured this perfume on My body, she did it to prepare Me for burial. 13 Truly I say to you, wherever this gospel is preached in the whole world, what this woman has done will also be spoken of in memory of her."

14 Then one of the twelve, named Judas Iscariot, went to the chief priests 15 and said, "What are you willing to give me to betray Him to you?" And they weighed out thirty pieces of silver to him. 16 From then on he *began* looking for a good opportunity to betray Jesus.

17 Now on the first *day* of Unleavened Bread the disciples came to Jesus and asked, "Where do You want us to prepare for You to eat the Passover?" 18 And He said, "Go into the city to a certain man, and say to

him, 'The Teacher says, "My time is near; I *am to* keep the Passover at your house with My disciples."'" [19] The disciples did as Jesus had directed them; and they prepared the Passover.

[20] Now when evening came, Jesus was reclining *at the table* with the twelve disciples. [21] As they were eating, He said, "Truly I say to you that one of you will betray Me." [22] Being deeply grieved, they each one began to say to Him, "Surely not I, Lord?" [23] And He answered, "He who dipped his hand with Me in the bowl is the one who will betray Me. [24] The Son of Man *is to* go, just as it is written of Him; but woe to that man by whom the Son of Man is betrayed! It would have been good for that man if he had not been born." [25] And Judas, who was betraying Him, said, "Surely it is not I, Rabbi?" Jesus said to him, "You have said *it* yourself."

[26] While they were eating, Jesus took *some* bread, and after a blessing, He broke *it* and gave *it* to the disciples, and said, "Take, eat; this is My body." [27] And when He had taken a cup and given thanks, He gave *it* to them, saying, "Drink from it, all of you; [28] for this is My blood of the covenant, which is poured out for many for forgiveness of sins. [29] But I say to you, I will not drink of this fruit of the vine from now on until that day when I drink it new with you in My Father's kingdom."

[30] After singing a hymn, they went out to the Mount of Olives.

[31] Then Jesus said to them, "You will all fall

away because of Me this night, for it is written, 'I
WILL STRIKE DOWN THE SHEPHERD, AND THE SHEEP OF
THE FLOCK SHALL BE SCATTERED.' ³² But after I have
been raised, I will go ahead of you to Galilee." ³³ But
Peter said to Him, "*Even* though all may fall away
because of You, I will never fall away." ³⁴ Jesus said to
him, "Truly I say to you that this *very* night, before a
rooster crows, you will deny Me three times." ³⁵ Peter
said to Him, "Even if I have to die with You, I will
not deny You." All the disciples said the same thing
too.

³⁶ Then Jesus came with them to a place called
Gethsemane, and said to His disciples, "Sit here while I
go over there and pray." ³⁷ And He took with Him Peter
and the two sons of Zebedee, and began to be grieved
and distressed. ³⁸ Then He said to them, "My soul is
deeply grieved, to the point of death; remain here and
keep watch with Me."

³⁹ And He went a little beyond *them*, and fell
on His face and prayed, saying, "My Father, if it is
possible, let this cup pass from Me; yet not as I will,
but as You will." ⁴⁰ And He came to the disciples
and found them sleeping, and said to Peter, "So, you
men could not keep watch with Me for one hour? ⁴¹
Keep watching and praying that you may not enter
into temptation; the spirit is willing, but the flesh is
weak."

⁴² He went away again a second time and
prayed, saying, "My Father, if this cannot pass away
unless I drink it, Your will be done." ⁴³ Again He

came and found them sleeping, for their eyes were heavy.

[44] And He left them again, and went away and prayed a third time, saying the same thing once more.

[45] Then He came to the disciples and said to them, "Are you still sleeping and resting? Behold, the hour is at hand and the Son of Man is being betrayed into the hands of sinners. [46] Get up, let us be going; behold, the one who betrays Me is at hand!"

[47] While He was still speaking, behold, Judas, one of the twelve, came up accompanied by a large crowd with swords and clubs, *who came* from the chief priests and elders of the people. [48] Now he who was betraying Him gave them a sign, saying, "Whomever I kiss, He is the one; seize Him." [49] Immediately Judas went to Jesus and said, "Hail, Rabbi!" and kissed Him. [50] And Jesus said to him, "Friend, *do* what you have come for." Then they came and laid hands on Jesus and seized Him.

[51] And behold, one of those who were with Jesus reached and drew out his sword, and struck the slave of the high priest and cut off his ear. [52] Then Jesus said to him, "Put your sword back into its place; for all those who take up the sword shall perish by the sword. [53] Or do you think that I cannot appeal to My Father, and He will at once put at My disposal more than twelve legions of angels? [54] How then will the Scriptures be fulfilled, *which say* that it must happen this way?"

⁵⁵ At that time Jesus said to the crowds, "Have you come out with swords and clubs to arrest Me as *you would* against a robber? Every day I used to sit in the temple teaching and you did not seize Me. ⁵⁶ But all this has taken place to fulfill the Scriptures of the prophets." Then all the disciples left Him and fled.

⁵⁷ Those who had seized Jesus led Him away to Caiaphas, the high priest, where the scribes and the elders were gathered together. ⁵⁸ But Peter was following Him at a distance as far as the courtyard of the high priest, and entered in, and sat down with the officers to see the outcome.

⁵⁹ Now the chief priests and the whole Council kept trying to obtain false testimony against Jesus, so that they might put Him to death. ⁶⁰ They did not find *any*, even though many false witnesses came forward. But later on two came forward, ⁶¹ and said, "This man stated, 'I am able to destroy the temple of God and to rebuild it in three days.'" ⁶² The high priest stood up and said to Him, "Do You not answer? What is it that these men are testifying against You?" ⁶³ But Jesus kept silent. And the high priest said to Him, "I adjure You by the living God, that You tell us whether You are the Christ, the Son of God." ⁶⁴ Jesus said to him, "You have said it *yourself*; nevertheless I tell you, hereafter you will see the Son of Man sitting at the right hand of Power, and coming on the clouds of heaven."

⁶⁵ Then the high priest tore his robes and said, "He has blasphemed! What further need do we

have of witnesses? Behold, you have now heard the blasphemy; 66 what do you think?" They answered, "He deserves death!"

67 Then they spat in His face and beat Him with their fists; and others slapped Him, 68 and said, "Prophesy to us, You Christ; who is the one who hit You?"

69 Now Peter was sitting outside in the courtyard, and a servant-girl came to him and said, "You too were with Jesus the Galilean." 70 But he denied it before them all, saying, "I do not know what you are talking about." 71 When he had gone out to the gateway, another *servant-girl* saw him and said to those who were there, "This man was with Jesus of Nazareth." 72 And again he denied it with an oath, "I do not know the man." 73 A little later the bystanders came up and said to Peter, "Surely you too are *one* of them; for even the way you talk gives you away." 74 Then he began to curse and swear, "I do not know the man!" And immediately a rooster crowed. 75 And Peter remembered the word which Jesus had said, "Before a rooster crows, you will deny Me three times." And he went out and wept bitterly.

Matthew 27 New American Standard Bible

1 Now when morning came, all the chief priests and the elders of the people conferred together against Jesus to put Him to death; 2 and they bound Him, and led Him away and delivered Him to Pilate the governor.

3 Then when Judas, who had betrayed Him, saw

that He had been condemned, he felt remorse and returned the thirty pieces of silver to the chief priests and elders, ⁴ saying, "I have sinned by betraying innocent blood." But they said, "What is that to us? See *to that* yourself!" ⁵ And he threw the pieces of silver into the temple sanctuary and departed; and he went away and hanged himself. ⁶ The chief priests took the pieces of silver and said, "It is not lawful to put them into the temple treasury, since it is the price of blood." ⁷ And they conferred together and with the money bought the Potter's Field as a burial place for strangers. ⁸ For this reason that field has been called the Field of Blood to this day. ⁹ Then that which was spoken through Jeremiah the prophet was fulfilled: "AND THEY TOOK THE THIRTY PIECES OF SILVER, THE PRICE OF THE ONE WHOSE PRICE HAD BEEN SET by the sons of Israel; ¹⁰ AND THEY GAVE THEM FOR THE POTTER'S FIELD, AS THE LORD DIRECTED ME."

¹¹ Now Jesus stood before the governor, and the governor questioned Him, saying, "Are You the King of the Jews?" And Jesus said to him, "*It is as you say.*" ¹² And while He was being accused by the chief priests and elders, He did not answer. ¹³ Then Pilate said to Him, "Do You not hear how many things they testify against You?" ¹⁴ And He did not answer him with regard to even a *single* charge, so the governor was quite amazed.

¹⁵ Now at *the* feast the governor was accustomed to release for the people *any* one prisoner whom they wanted. ¹⁶ At that time they were holding a notorious

prisoner, called Barabbas. [17] So when the people gathered together, Pilate said to them, "Whom do you want me to release for you? Barabbas, or Jesus who is called Christ?" [18] For he knew that because of envy they had handed Him over.

[19] While he was sitting on the judgment seat, his wife sent him *a message*, saying, "Have nothing to do with that righteous Man; for last night I suffered greatly in a dream because of Him." [20] But the chief priests and the elders persuaded the crowds to ask for Barabbas and to put Jesus to death. [21] But the governor said to them, "Which of the two do you want me to release for you?" And they said, "Barabbas." [22] Pilate said to them, "Then what shall I do with Jesus who is called Christ?" They all said, "Crucify Him!" [23] And he said, "Why, what evil has He done?" But they kept shouting all the more, saying, "Crucify Him!"

[24] When Pilate saw that he was accomplishing nothing, but rather that a riot was starting, he took water and washed his hands in front of the crowd, saying, "I am innocent of this Man's blood; see *to that* yourselves." [25] And all the people said, "His blood shall be on us and on our children!" [26] Then he released Barabbas for them; but after having Jesus scourged, he handed Him over to be crucified.

[27] Then the soldiers of the governor took Jesus into the Praetorium and gathered the whole *Roman* cohort around Him. [28] They stripped Him and put a scarlet robe on Him. [29] And after twisting together a

crown of thorns, they put it on His head, and a reed
in His right hand; and they knelt down before Him
and mocked Him, saying, "Hail, King of the Jews!"
³⁰ They spat on Him, and took the reed and *began*
to beat Him on the head. ³¹ After they had mocked
Him, they took the *scarlet* robe off Him and put His
own garments back on Him, and led Him away to
crucify Him.

³² As they were coming out, they found a man
of Cyrene named Simon, whom they pressed into
service to bear His cross.

³³ And when they came to a place called
Golgotha, which means Place of a Skull, ³⁴ they gave
Him wine to drink mixed with gall; and after tasting
it, He was unwilling to drink.

³⁵ And when they had crucified Him, they
divided up His garments among themselves by
casting lots. ³⁶ And sitting down, they *began* to keep
watch over Him there. ³⁷ And above His head they
put up the charge against Him which read, "THIS IS
JESUS THE KING OF THE JEWS."

³⁸ At that time two robbers were crucified with
Him, one on the right and one on the left. ³⁹ And
those passing by were hurling abuse at Him, wagging
their heads ⁴⁰ and saying, "You who *are going to*
destroy the temple and rebuild it in three days, save
Yourself! If You are the Son of God, come down
from the cross." ⁴¹ In the same way the chief priests
also, along with the scribes and elders, were mocking
Him and saying, ⁴² "He saved others; He cannot save

Himself. He is the King of Israel; let Him now come
down from the cross, and we will believe in Him.
⁴³ HE TRUSTS IN GOD; LET GOD RESCUE *Him* now, IF HE
DELIGHTS IN HIM; for He said, 'I am the Son of God.'"
⁴⁴ The robbers who had been crucified with Him
were also insulting Him with the same words.

⁴⁵ Now from the sixth hour darkness fell upon
all the land until the ninth hour. ⁴⁶ About the ninth
hour Jesus cried out with a loud voice, saying, "ELI,
ELI, LAMA SABACHTHANI?" that is, "MY GOD, MY
GOD, WHY HAVE YOU FORSAKEN ME?" ⁴⁷ And some
of those who were standing there, when they heard
it, *began* saying, "This man is calling for Elijah." ⁴⁸
Immediately one of them ran, and taking a sponge,
he filled it with sour wine and put it on a reed, and
gave Him a drink. ⁴⁹ But the rest *of them* said, "Let us
see whether Elijah will come to save Him." ⁵⁰ And
Jesus cried out again with a loud voice, and yielded
up His spirit. ⁵¹ And behold, the veil of the temple
was torn in two from top to bottom; and the earth
shook and the rocks were split. ⁵² The tombs were
opened, and many bodies of the saints who had
fallen asleep were raised; ⁵³ and coming out of the
tombs after His resurrection they entered the holy
city and appeared to many. ⁵⁴ Now the centurion,
and those who were with him keeping guard over
Jesus, when they saw the earthquake and the things
that were happening, became very frightened and
said, "Truly this was the Son of God!"

⁵⁵ Many women were there looking on from

a distance, who had followed Jesus from Galilee while ministering to Him. [56] Among them was Mary Magdalene, and Mary the mother of James and Joseph, and the mother of the sons of Zebedee.

[57] When it was evening, there came a rich man from Arimathea, named Joseph, who himself had also become a disciple of Jesus. [58] This man went to Pilate and asked for the body of Jesus. Then Pilate ordered it to be given *to him*. [59] And Joseph took the body and wrapped it in a clean linen cloth, [60] and laid it in his own new tomb, which he had hewn out in the rock; and he rolled a large stone against the entrance of the tomb and went away. [61] And Mary Magdalene was there, and the other Mary, sitting opposite the grave.

[62] Now on the next day, the day after the preparation, the chief priests and the Pharisees gathered together with Pilate, [63] and said, "Sir, we remember that when He was still alive that deceiver said, 'After three days I *am to* rise again.' [64] Therefore, give orders for the grave to be made secure until the third day, otherwise His disciples may come and steal Him away and say to the people, 'He has risen from the dead,' and the last deception will be worse than the first." [65] Pilate said to them, "You have a guard; go, make it *as* secure as you know how." [66] And they went and made the grave secure, and along with the guard they set a seal on the stone.

Matthew 28 New American Standard Bible
[1] Now after the Sabbath, as it began to dawn

toward the first *day* of the week, Mary Magdalene and the other Mary came to look at the grave. ² And behold, a severe earthquake had occurred, for an angel of the Lord descended from heaven and came and rolled away the stone and sat upon it. ³ And his appearance was like lightning, and his clothing as white as snow. ⁴ The guards shook for fear of him and became like dead men. ⁵ The angel said to the women, "Do not be afraid; for I know that you are looking for Jesus who has been crucified. ⁶ He is not here, for He has risen, just as He said. Come, see the place where He was lying. ⁷ Go quickly and tell His disciples that He has risen from the dead; and behold, He is going ahead of you into Galilee, there you will see Him; behold, I have told you."

⁸ And they left the tomb quickly with fear and great joy and ran to report it to His disciples. ⁹ And behold, Jesus met them and greeted them. And they came up and took hold of His feet and worshiped Him. ¹⁰ Then Jesus said to them, "Do not be afraid; go and take word to My brethren to leave for Galilee, and there they will see Me."

¹¹ Now while they were on their way, some of the guard came into the city and reported to the chief priests all that had happened. ¹² And when they had assembled with the elders and consulted together, they gave a large sum of money to the soldiers, ¹³ and said, "You are to say, 'His disciples came by night and stole Him away while we were asleep.' ¹⁴ And if this should come to the governor's ears, we

will win him over and keep you out of trouble." [15] And they took the money and did as they had been instructed; and this story was widely spread among the Jews, *and is* to this day.

[16] But the eleven disciples proceeded to Galilee, to the mountain which Jesus had designated. [17] When they saw Him, they worshiped *Him*; but some were doubtful. [18] And Jesus came up and spoke to them, saying, "All authority has been given to Me in heaven and on earth. [19] Go therefore and make disciples of all the nations, baptizing them in the name of the Father and the Son and the Holy Spirit, [20] teaching them to observe all that I commanded you; and lo, I am with you always, even to the end of the age."

Acts 1:1-5, 8-9; 2:1-18, 21 NEW INTERNATIONAL VERSION

[1] In my former book, Theophilus, I wrote about all that Jesus began to do and to teach [2] until the day he was taken up to heaven, after giving instructions through the Holy Spirit to the apostles he had chosen. [3] After his suffering, he presented himself to them and gave many convincing proofs that he was alive. He appeared to them over a period of forty days and spoke about the kingdom of God. [4] On one occasion, while he was eating with them, he gave them this command: "Do not leave Jerusalem, but wait for the gift my Father promised, which you have heard me speak about. [5] For John baptized with water, but in a few days you will be baptized with the Holy Spirit."

[8] "But you will receive power when the Holy Spirit comes on you; and you will be my witnesses in Jerusalem, and in all Judea and Samaria, and to the ends of the earth."

[9] After he said this, he was taken up before their very eyes, and a cloud hid him from their sight.

[1] When the day of Pentecost came, they were all together in one place. [2] Suddenly a sound like the blowing of a violent wind came from heaven and filled the whole house where they were sitting. [3] They saw what seemed to be tongues of fire that separated and came to rest on each of them. [4] All of them were filled with the Holy Spirit and began to speak in other tongues as the Spirit enabled them.

[5] Now there were staying in Jerusalem God-fearing Jews from every nation under heaven. [6] When they heard this sound, a crowd came together in bewilderment, because each one heard their own language being spoken. [7] Utterly amazed, they asked: "Aren't all these who are speaking Galileans? [8] Then how is it that each of us hears them in our native language? [9] Parthians, Medes and Elamites; residents of Mesopotamia, Judea and Cappadocia, Pontus and Asia, [10] Phrygia and Pamphylia, Egypt and the parts of Libya near Cyrene; visitors from Rome [11] (both Jews and converts to Judaism); Cretans and Arabs— we hear them declaring the wonders of God in our own tongues!" [12] Amazed and perplexed, they asked one another, "What does this mean?"

[13] Some, however, made fun of them and said,

"They have had too much wine."

¹⁴ Then Peter stood up with the Eleven, raised his voice and addressed the crowd: "Fellow Jews and all of you who live in Jerusalem, let me explain this to you; listen carefully to what I say. ¹⁵ These people are not drunk, as you suppose. It's only nine in the morning! ¹⁶ No, this is what was spoken by the prophet Joel:

¹⁷ "'In the last days, God says,
   I will pour out my Spirit on all people.
Your sons and daughters will prophesy,
   your young men will see visions,
   your old men will dream dreams.
¹⁸ Even on my servants, both men and women,
   I will pour out my Spirit in those days,
   and they will prophesy.
²¹ And everyone who calls
   on the name of the Lord will be saved.'"

9 • *the truth*

Matthew 28:18-20

¹⁸ And Jesus came and spoke to them, saying, "All authority has been given to Me in heaven and on earth. ¹⁹ Go therefore and make disciples of all the nations, baptizing them in the name of the Father and of the Son and of the Holy Spirit, ²⁰ teaching them to observe all things that I have commanded you; and lo, I am with you always, *even* to the end of the age." Amen.

Mark 16:15-20

¹⁵ And He said to them, "Go into all the world and preach the gospel to every creature. ¹⁶ He who believes and is baptized will be saved; but he who does not believe will be condemned. ¹⁷ And these signs will follow those who believe: In My name they will cast out demons; they will speak with new tongues; ¹⁸ they will take up serpents; and if they drink anything deadly, it will by no means hurt them; they will lay hands on the sick, and they will recover."

¹⁹ So then, after the Lord had spoken to them, He was received up into heaven, and sat down at the right hand of God. ²⁰ And they went out and preached everywhere, the Lord working with *them* and confirming the word through the accompanying signs. Amen.

Acts 2:1-21 NEW INTERNATIONAL VERSION

¹ When the day of Pentecost came, they were all together in one place. ² Suddenly a sound like the blowing of a violent wind came from heaven and filled the whole house where they were sitting. ³ They saw what seemed to be tongues of fire that separated and came to rest on each of them. ⁴ All of them were filled with the Holy Spirit and began to speak in other tongues as the Spirit enabled them.

⁵ Now there were staying in Jerusalem God-fearing Jews from every nation under heaven. ⁶ When they heard this sound, a crowd came together in bewilderment, because each one heard their own

language being spoken. [7] Utterly amazed, they asked: "Aren't all these who are speaking Galileans? [8] Then how is it that each of us hears them in our native language? [9] Parthians, Medes and Elamites; residents of Mesopotamia, Judea and Cappadocia, Pontus and Asia, [10] Phrygia and Pamphylia, Egypt and the parts of Libya near Cyrene; visitors from Rome [11] (both Jews and converts to Judaism); Cretans and Arabs— we hear them declaring the wonders of God in our own tongues!" [12] Amazed and perplexed, they asked one another, "What does this mean?"

[13] Some, however, made fun of them and said, "They have had too much wine."

John 8:43-44 New American Standard Bible

[43] Why do you not understand what I am saying? *It is* because you cannot hear My word. [44] You are of *your* father the devil, and you want to do the desires of your father. He was a murderer from the beginning, and does not stand in the truth because there is no truth in him. Whenever he speaks a lie, he speaks from his own *nature*, for he is a liar and the father of lies.

2 Corinthians 4:3-4 The Living Bible

[3] If the Good News we preach is hidden to anyone, it is hidden from the one who is on the road to eternal death. [4] Satan, who is the god of this evil world, has made him blind, unable to see the glorious light of the Gospel that is shining upon him or to understand the amazing message we preach about the glory of Christ, who is God.

Luke 10:17-19

[17] Then the seventy returned with joy, saying, "Lord, even the demons are subject to us in Your name."

[18] And He said to them, "I saw Satan fall like lightning from heaven. [19] Behold, I give you the authority to trample on serpents and scorpions, and over all the power of the enemy, and nothing shall by any means hurt you.

John 1:1-3, 14, 17

[1] In the beginning was the Word, and the Word was with God, and the Word was God. [2] He was in the beginning with God. [3] All things were made through Him, and without Him nothing was made that was made.

[14] And the Word became flesh and dwelt among us, and we beheld His glory, the glory as of the only begotten of the Father, full of grace and truth.

[17] For the law was given through Moses, *but* grace and truth came through Jesus Christ.

John 17:17 New Living Translation

Make them holy by your truth; teach them your word, which is truth.

Hebrews 13:8

Jesus Christ *is* the same yesterday, today, and forever.

10 • *the life*

2 Corinthians 5:17

Therefore, if anyone *is* in Christ, *he is* a new creation; old things have passed away; behold, all things have become new.

John 1:4

In Him was life, and the life was the light of men.

1 John 1:1-2 NEW LIVING TRANSLATION

[1] We proclaim to you the one who existed from the beginning, whom we have heard and seen. We saw him with our own eyes and touched him with our own hands. He is the Word of life. [2] This one who is life itself was revealed to us, and we have seen him. And now we testify and proclaim to you that he is the one who is eternal life.

1 Corinthians 15:45

And so it is written, "The first man Adam became a living being." The last Adam [Jesus] *became* a life-giving spirit.

John 3:1-8

[1] There was a man of the Pharisees named Nicodemus, a ruler of the Jews. [2] This man came to Jesus by night and said to Him, "Rabbi, we know that You are a teacher come from God; for no one can do these signs that You do unless God is with him."

[3] Jesus answered and said to him, "Most assuredly, I say to you, unless one is born again, he

cannot see the kingdom of God."

⁴ Nicodemus said to Him, "How can a man be born when he is old? Can he enter a second time into his mother's womb and be born?"

⁵ Jesus answered, "Most assuredly, I say to you, unless one is born of water and the Spirit, he cannot enter the kingdom of God. ⁶ That which is born of the flesh is flesh, and that which is born of the Spirit is spirit. ⁷ Do not marvel that I said to you, 'You must be born again.' ⁸ The wind blows where it wishes, and you hear the sound of it, but cannot tell where it comes from and where it goes. So is everyone who is born of the Spirit."

Ezekiel 36:26-27

²⁶ I will give you a new heart and put a new spirit within you; I will take the heart of stone out of your flesh and give you a heart of flesh. ²⁷ I will put My Spirit within you and cause you to walk in My statutes, and you will keep My judgments and do *them.*

John 14:26

But the Helper, the Holy Spirit, whom the Father will send in My name, He will teach you all things, and bring to your remembrance all things that I said to you.

Acts 1:8

"But you shall receive power when the Holy Spirit has come upon you; and you shall be witnesses to Me in Jerusalem, and in all Judea and Samaria, and to the end of the earth."

Galatians 5:16

I say then: Walk in the Spirit, and you shall not fulfill the lust of the flesh.

Philippians 3:20

For our citizenship is in heaven.

Colossians 1:3-5

[3] We give thanks to the God and Father of our Lord Jesus Christ, praying always for you, [4] since we heard of your faith in Christ Jesus and of your love for all the saints; [5] because of the hope which is laid up for you in heaven, of which you heard before in the word of the truth of the gospel.

John 16:33

"These things I have spoken to you, that in Me you may have peace. In the world you will have tribulation; but be of good cheer, I have overcome the world."

Matthew 19:26

But Jesus looked at *them* and said to them, "With men this is impossible, but with God all things are possible."

Romans 8:31

If God is for us, who can be against us?

11 • *the most important decision ever*

Romans 10:8-10

[8] But what does it say? "The word is near you, in your mouth and in your heart" (that is, the word of faith which we preach): [9] that if you confess with

your mouth the Lord Jesus and believe in your heart that God has raised Him from the dead, you will be saved. [10] For with the heart one believes unto righteousness, and with the mouth confession is made unto salvation.

Romans 5:8

But God demonstrates His own love toward us, in that while we were still sinners, Christ died for us.

John 3:16-17

[16] For God so loved the world that He gave His only begotten Son, that whoever believes in Him should not perish but have everlasting life. [17] For God did not send His Son into the world to condemn the world, but that the world through Him might be saved.

Colossians 2:13-15 New Century Version

[13] When you were spiritually dead because of your sins and because you were not free from the power of your sinful self, God made you alive with Christ, and he forgave all our sins. [14] He canceled the debt, which listed all the rules we failed to follow. He took away that record with its rules and nailed it to the cross. [15] God stripped the spiritual rulers and powers [evil spirits] of their authority. With the cross, he won the victory and showed the world that they were powerless.

Luke 10:18-20

[18] And He said to them, "I saw Satan fall like lightning from heaven. [19] Behold, I give you the

authority to trample on serpents and scorpions, and over all the power of the enemy, and nothing shall by any means hurt you. [20] Nevertheless do not rejoice in this, that the spirits are subject to you, but rather rejoice because your names are written in heaven."

Hebrews 2:3

How shall we escape if we neglect so great a salvation, which at the first began to be spoken by the Lord, and was confirmed to us by those who heard *Him?*

Romans 10:17

So then faith *comes* by hearing, and hearing by the word of God.

1 Corinthians 15:1-5

Moreover, brethren, I declare to you the gospel which I preached to you, which also you received and in which you stand, [2] by which also you are saved, if you hold fast that word which I preached to you—unless you believed in vain. [3] For I delivered to you first of all that which I also received: that Christ died for our sins according to the Scriptures, and [4] that He was buried, and that He rose again the third day according to the Scriptures, [5] and that He was seen by Cephas, then by the twelve.

12 • if . . . then

Luke 15:10

"Likewise, I say to you, there is joy in the presence

of the angels of God over one sinner who repents."

Galatians 4:6

And because you are sons, God has sent forth the Spirit of His Son into your hearts, crying out, "Abba, Father!"

1 Corinthians 12:12-27 New Living Translation

[12] The human body has many parts, but the many parts make up one whole body. So it is with the body of Christ. [13] Some of us are Jews, some are Gentiles, some are slaves, and some are free. But we have all been baptized into one body by one Spirit, and we all share the same Spirit.

[14] Yes, the body has many different parts, not just one part. [15] If the foot says, "I am not a part of the body because I am not a hand," that does not make it any less a part of the body. [16] And if the ear says, "I am not part of the body because I am not an eye," would that make it any less a part of the body? [17] If the whole body were an eye, how would you hear? Or if your whole body were an ear, how would you smell anything?

[18] But our bodies have many parts, and God has put each part just where he wants it. [19] How strange a body would be if it had only one part! [20] Yes, there are many parts, but only one body. [21] The eye can never say to the hand, "I don't need you." The head can't say to the feet, "I don't need you."

[22] In fact, some parts of the body that seem weakest and least important are actually the most necessary. [23] And the parts we regard as less

honorable are those we clothe with the greatest care. So we carefully protect those parts that should not be seen, [24] while the more honorable parts do not require this special care. So God has put the body together such that extra honor and care are given to those parts that have less dignity. [25] This makes for harmony among the members, so that all the members care for each other. [26] If one part suffers, all the parts suffer with it, and if one part is honored, all the parts are glad.

[27] All of you together are Christ's body, and each of you is a part of it.

Ephesians 4:11-16 New Living Translation

[11] Now these are the gifts Christ gave to the church: the apostles, the prophets, the evangelists, and the pastors and teachers. [12] Their responsibility is to equip God's people to do his work and build up the church, the body of Christ. [13] This will continue until we all come to such unity in our faith and knowledge of God's Son that we will be mature in the Lord, measuring up to the full and complete standard of Christ.

[14] Then we will no longer be immature like children. We won't be tossed and blown about by every wind of new teaching. We will not be influenced when people try to trick us with lies so clever they sound like the truth. [15] Instead, we will speak the truth in love, growing in every way more and more like Christ, who is the head of his body, the church. [16] He makes the whole body fit together

perfectly. As each part does its own special work, it helps the other parts grow, so that the whole body is healthy and growing and full of love.

Hebrews 10:24-25

[24] And let us consider one another in order to stir up love and good works, [25] not forsaking the assembling of ourselves together, as *is* the manner of some, but exhorting *one another*, and so much the more as you see the Day approaching.

Romans 12:4-8 New Living Translation

[4] Just as our bodies have many parts and each part has a special function, [5] so it is with Christ's body. We are many parts of one body, and we all belong to each other.

[6] In his grace, God has given us different gifts for doing certain things well. So if God has given you the ability to prophesy, speak out with as much faith as God has given you. [7] If your gift is serving others, serve them well. If you are a teacher, teach well. [8] If your gift is to encourage others, be encouraging. If it is giving, give generously. If God has given you leadership ability, take the responsibility seriously. And if you have a gift for showing kindness to others, do it gladly.

Galatians 5:22-23 New Living Translation

[22] But the Holy Spirit produces this kind of fruit in our lives: love, joy, peace, patience, kindness, goodness, faithfulness, [23] gentleness, and self-control. There is no law against these things!

Romans 6:3-5

³ Or do you not know that as many of us as were baptized into Christ Jesus were baptized into His death? ⁴ Therefore we were buried with Him through baptism into death, that just as Christ was raised from the dead by the glory of the Father, even so we also should walk in newness of life.

⁵ For if we have been united together in the likeness of His death, certainly we also shall be *in the likeness* of *His* resurrection.

Acts 2:4 New American Standard Bible

And they were all filled with the Holy Spirit and began to speak with other tongues, as the Spirit was giving them utterance.

Acts 2:38-39 New Living Translation

³⁸ Peter replied, "Each of you must repent of your sins and turn to God, and be baptized in the name of Jesus Christ for the forgiveness of your sins. Then you will receive the gift of the Holy Spirit. ³⁹ This promise is to you, to your children, and to those far away—all who have been called by the Lord our God."

Acts 10:44-48 New American Standard Bible

⁴⁴ While Peter was still speaking these words, the Holy Spirit fell upon all those who were listening to the message. ⁴⁵ All the circumcised believers who came with Peter were amazed, because the gift of the Holy Spirit had been poured out on the Gentiles also. ⁴⁶ For they were hearing them speaking with tongues and exalting God. Then Peter answered,

[47] "Surely no one can refuse the water for these to be baptized who have received the Holy Spirit just as we *did*, can he?" [48] And he ordered them to be baptized in the name of Jesus Christ. Then they asked him to stay on for a few days.

Acts 19:1-6 New American Standard Bible

[1] It happened that while Apollos was at Corinth, Paul passed through the upper country and came to Ephesus, and found some disciples. [2] He said to them, "Did you receive the Holy Spirit when you believed?" And they *said* to him, "No, we have not even heard whether there is a Holy Spirit." [3] And he said, "Into what then were you baptized?" And they said, "Into John's baptism." [4] Paul said, "John baptized with the baptism of repentance, telling the people to believe in Him who was coming after him, that is, in Jesus." [5] When they heard this, they were baptized in the name of the Lord Jesus. [6] And when Paul had laid his hands upon them, the Holy Spirit came on them, and they *began* speaking with tongues and prophesying.

1 Corinthians 14:21

In the law it is written:
"With *men of* other tongues and other lips
I will speak to this people."

Mark 16:17-18

[17] "And these signs will follow those who believe: In My name they will cast out demons; they will speak with new tongues; [18] they will take up serpents; and if they drink anything deadly, it will by

no means hurt them; they will lay hands on the sick, and they will recover."

Jude 20-21

[20] But you, beloved, building yourselves up on your most holy faith, praying in the Holy Spirit, [21] keep yourselves in the love of God, looking for the mercy of our Lord Jesus Christ unto eternal life.

1 Thessalonians 5:17

Pray without ceasing.

John 8:31-32

[31] Then Jesus said to those Jews who believed Him, "If you abide in My word, you are My disciples indeed. [32] And you shall know the truth, and the truth shall make you free."

2 Timothy 2:15 NEW INTERNATIONAL VERSION

Do your best to present yourself to God as one approved, a worker who does not need to be ashamed and who correctly handles the word of truth.

Romans 12:1-2 NEW LIVING TRANSLATION

[1] And so, dear brothers and sisters, I plead with you to give your bodies to God because of all he has done for you. Let them be a living and holy sacrifice—the kind he will find acceptable. This is truly the way to worship him. [2] Don't copy the behavior and customs of this world, but let God transform you into a new person by changing the way you think. Then you will learn to know God's will for you, which is good and pleasing and perfect.

John 15:15

"No longer do I call you servants, for a servant does not know what his master is doing; but I have called you friends, for all things that I heard from My Father I have made known to you."

Galatians 2:20

I have been crucified with Christ; it is no longer I who live, but Christ lives in me; and the *life* which I now live in the flesh I live by faith in the Son of God, who loved me and gave Himself for me.

Bible translation credit lines

R.J. Albanese graduated from the University of Virginia hoping to capture the American Dream on many fronts. He found success as an executive in a computer software company, and he also found artistic fulfillment through performing in a rock 'n' roll band. Yet, these achievements were hollow victories. Something was missing. Realizing his life lacked purpose, he set out to find the meaning of life. His extensive quest revealed the indisputable answer, which transformed his life forever.

to order more books
or download them
go to:

www.rjalbanese.com

www.ingramcontent.com/pod-product-compliance
Lightning Source LLC
Chambersburg PA
CBHW070729130626
46553CB00005B/2214